ANCHOR BOOKS

INSPIRATIONS FROM

NORTHERN IRELAND

Edited by

David Foskett

First published in Great Britain in 1996 by
ANCHOR BOOKS
1-2 Wainman Road, Woodston,
Peterborough, PE2 7BU

HB ISBN 1 85930 338 2
SB ISBN 1 85930 333 1

Foreword

Anchor Books is a small press, established in 1992, with the aim of promoting readable poetry to as wide an audience as possible.

The poems in *Inspirations From Northern Ireland* represent a cross-section of style and content.

These poems are written by young and old alike, united in their passion for writing poetry.

I trust this selection will delight and please the authors from *Northern Ireland* and all those who enjoy reading poetry.

David Foskett
Editor

CONTENTS

INCH CASTLE

Dusk is fighting against the dwindling light,
The castle looms, and from the lough,
A raw, imposing sight.
The moon is up and rises overhead,
I hear the ghosts of yesteryear cry out,
The O Doherty is dead.

She comes to me wailing in the wind,
Her lament crying vengeance from the shore,
Steady she sits and combs her rugged hair,
Alas! O Doherty is no more.

Sleep comes upon me, too soon arrives the dawn,
The sullen call of the curlew,
As he wakes from troubled sleep,
The castle lies in ruins, with ivy on its throne,
Alas once the ruling place,
Of the Prince of Inishowen.

Paul Devlin

A DIFFERENT COSMOS

The ale pumps are my Northern Lights.
The optics are the stars,
And the barmaid is the satellite
Orbiting the fake oak bar.

Conversations drone as an autumn gale,
Whisk past my deadened ears.
I barely catch an old friend's hail,
Yet raise a glass in cheers.

Still visions of the past intrude,
Dread, dead, glimpses of that smile.
How could she have misunderstood?
Loss? I gulp that bitter bile.

Now the beer brings dissipation.
Now I can laugh and joke because
I am spared love's contemplation
For a while . . . in a different cosmos.

Perry McDaid

SLIEVENAMAN

As I gaze o'er the valley - a patchwork of green
The haystacks are built and the fields are now clean
The hedges are white with the blossom of May
And the scent fills the air at the close of the day:
Men and women devoted their lives to this land
These farmlands and homesteads were formed by their hand
The ditches of stone that withstand wind and rain
As a tribute to hardship and labour remain.
The mountains of purple that stretch to the sky
Contrast with the forests of pine trees so high -
Whether clouds throw their shadow or the sun it does shine
There's such pride in my heart for this country of mine.
The Slievenaman Valley with her treasures untold
More precious by far than silver or gold
Form an overall picture of beauty supreme
Encaptured and held in my heart like a dream
As we walk on these paths which our forefathers trod -
Feel the peace, the contentment, the closeness to God.

Iris Corbett

3 PEACES - 3 PIECES

The peace of the night,
The peace of the heavenly sky
The peace of the morn
The thump inside those
who need to mourn.

The buzz of the day, yet
the children aren't safe at play
At the close of the eve -
when some conceive
to play in the dark like
a wide mouthed shark.

It's prayer,
Not despair,
Peace has died
Peace is risen
Peace will come again.

Mary Aigneis Murphy

REBIRTH OF DERRY

The bells toll for hope
They toll for departed pity
Of the rebirth of this once proud city
Barbed wire no longer pricks the skyline
And children play in the winter sunshine
The walls are open once again
Their secret belies so much pain
Of battles fought
Of tempers fraught
There is a new hope in the Derry air
Which once captured so much despair
Decimated metal has been replaced
By the cooing of doves which have come to settle
Tourists flourish here now
To see the history and its holy row
Rekindling memories of Lundy
Of internment and Bloody Sunday
And as the city approaches a new world order
One prays it will no longer return to civil disorder.

Finnan Boyle

UNTITLED

I am often reminded
At the beginning of the year
When I had to enter the 'City'
No doubt with a little fear.

Soon to arrive was a doctor
Welcomed to this wonderful place
A very attractive redhead
With a smile on her radiant face.

Being later moved to a large ward
In the company of three other
Making friends with this lot
To me is was no bother.

Everywhere, spotlessly clean and cosy
Everything spick and span
The cleaners do a daily job
That would please any man.

The catering staff always welcome
They fairly toe the line
The food served, very tasty
And always in good time.

Doctors and nurses are exceptional
With never a single frown
Whether being from the country
Or in the heart of town.

All so neat and tidy
My word, they do look well
Always doing their utmost
To make sure everyone's well.

If you're down and on the losing side
Take a tip from me
Put your all on the 'Mighty City'
A sure winner, you will be.

T J Warren

THE SEASON OF BEAUTY AND GLEE

Snowflakes falling silently
Weaving a carpet intricately,
Dazzling white so soft and deep
Soon to be ruined by trodden feet.

Prints embedded in the snow showing where
the people go,
Branches glisten from morn till night,
Naturally green, but prettier white.

Snowmen standing here and there getting
fatter with every layer,
Dreading the thaw with all their might
Melting them down till they're out of sight.

Icicles hanging from roof tops
Sparkle like crystal in the jeweller's shop,
Robins hopping on the ground
Hoping a crust or some crumbs can be found.

Children dressed in woollies bright
Guarding from Jack's nips and bites,
Fur lined boots for the snow so deep,
Wellingtons for slush and sleet.

Fairy lights on Christmas trees
A prettier sight you never will see,
Children busy writing letters
To Santa Claus and his little helpers.

Holly, ivy and mistletoe
Pretty presents wrapped with bows,
Robins pecking on the sill
Throughout the season of goodwill.

I call it the season of beauty and glee
Full of happiness and tranquillity,
The prettiest season of the year
Full of beauty and Christmas cheer.

Marie Elliott

FOR MY GRANDFATHER

My Grandfather's hands had once cut turf
beautifully
Their skin taut and smooth as a stone
His pleated fingers gathered me to him
And my childish face fitted neatly in their
folds.

When he laughed,
I bathed in the sunny echoes of his joy
When he cried,
I searched for him
When he was angry,
Black as the night was his rage
But when he forgave
yellow and fragrant as his rose garden
was my redemption.

Now when I see an old man
Rise and fall among his flower beds,
A small girl big-eyed by his side,
His thoughts and mine seem to mingle together
And I smile and am glad.
That you were always there
To be my father.

Michelle Magennis

THE SEA

Looking out to the broad wild sea,
As free, as free, as free as can be,
No one can say to he 'be halt',
And stop him producing his treasure's and salt.

He rides his white horse from the depths to the Docks,
And powerfully collides with the denseness of rocks,
Green and blue such colours of force,
Tide in, tide out committing his duties on his eternal
course.

You can hear him talk, laugh and cry,
and see him hold hands with his wife, our sky
from shoreline to shoreline is his own,
Our dear sea, is life's backbone.

Jonathan Leddy

PEACEFUL DERRY

Derry in the early morning
While the dew is still falling
Is a peaceful place
Full of silence
Full of grace
Looking down onto the river
I feel a gentle breeze
Which makes me shiver
Then I walk for a little while
And I hear a little bird singing
Which makes me smile
And I think
This is home.

Joseph Moore

FREEDOM

At last we are free, free from violence.
We are free from the armoured cars,
the bombed out bars of that terrible war.
Catholics and Protestants alike went out to fight
for different things, but the same things.

Now they know that war is wrong,
as they try to work things out,
Will we return to war, or stay at peace.
Which was always just out of reach.

As the politicians work to bring all sides together.
We are uncertain that they can do it.
What is the problem? Why not go on?
The answer is the threat of the *bomb*.

Hand in the arms. Take out the armoured cars.
Bring *peace* to our country.
We want to be free from hate and misunderstanding.
Let the politicians talk and get us what we lust for.

Gerard Moore

A RUNNER IN DERRY CITY

Thirteen years and two months, but who's counting?
That's how long I spent in you.
When nobody else would give me a job
Derry city offered me two.
To barricades, bullets and bombs I arrived,
Fresh from college in seventy-three.
If a school inspector was likely to call
Was the uppermost worry with me.

In my thirteenth winter a colleague from school,
Insisted I should meet her mother.
I was covered in snow and preferred not to go,
But I went in to save any bother.
'This is Clare, she is from Ballycastle.'
(I prepared for the Lammas Fair jokes).
Instead she complained, 'I think it's a shame,
You runners steal jobs from the poor Derry folks!'

They say that your life flashes past you
Before you are going to die.
I didn't drop dead, but it must be said
At that time thirteen years did flash by!
I thought of the hundreds of children I'd taught,
And the friends that I'd made through the years,
(In particular the fellow from Francis Street).
I thought of the laughter and tears.

I was too shocked that day to give an answer,
But the answer I give now is true.
Derry city, I was *more* than a runner,
I did so much living in you.

Clare McAfee

A TIME OF INNOCENCE

In their eyes, there lurks a sadness
which no-one can understand
this is because the way in which
their poverty-stricken land
has been abandoned by everyone
who used to know it well
and now these people consider it
as a living hell.

In the land of skeletons
thousands die each day
all the parents can do
is look on in dismay
they cannot hide their grief
as tears roll down their face
there are no headstones, there are no graves
there are no memories for them to save.

At last they get some food
although it does not taste so good
they want to have a family meal
and know how other families feel
to see their children enjoying food
to see them in a healthy state
not to see them waste away
when they do not live another day.

Eileen Black

DANCE OF FREEDOM?

I watched in fascination
As it twirled and swirled around,
Soaring high into the air -
Then falling to the ground,
It lay there for a while -
No movement could I see,
Then suddenly, it's in the air
In a frenzied dance of glee,
I watched it thro' my window pane
Wiped clear - the better to see
That little golden, gale-blown leaf -
Which had once adorned a tree.

Betty Adams-Mailey

ARMAGH

A city of infinite beauty,
Of cultural and celestial joy,
Endowed with haunting historical heritage,
A tranquil treasure amidst a sea of turmoil.

It's borne the pain of decades,
Remaining steadfast and strong,
When its structures have crashed and crumbled,
It's bravely began to build again and carry on.

Its courage and faith are unbounding,
Its strength eternal and true,
It personifies all that at times we are lacking,
An inspiration to me and to you.

Nature has a profound prominence here,
Especially the trees which wordlessly whisper,
They have so many secrets to tell,
Of Armagh the precious city where they do dwell.

The Mall which is glorified by creation,
Is a sacred lovers' retreat,
The beauty it conveys with each passing season,
Touches the hearts of all I meet.

Armagh is a city of history and honour,
Exuding warmth and love,
A portrait of promise and peace,
A shining beacon of hope for the future.

Katharine Emily Bell

UNTITLED

In an old country churchyard,
its weary earth long undisturbed by boots on spades,
October gusts send leaves of Autumn hues
scuttling along the silent stone guardians
of abandoned identities.
In this village of weed-choked tombs and crypts
perching rooks and dry academics
are the only visitors.
No face to put to a name
as they scan indifferently the moss dirty letters
once chiselled so skilfully by calloused hands
on these redundant memorials
to men and women long departed
from life and from the living
as those they left behind,
and trusted to remember,
also turned their faces to the wall
and forgot.

John Metrustry

CONSERVATION?

We are the destroyers;
Requiring more roads, more oil, more photocopies,
Year by year.
Wildlife, meadows and forests disappear
To satisfy our needs.
We cannot possibly put back
All that we have taken.
A few among the millions understand;
They know that we must stop and think and plan,
Stop caring only for the here and now
And think about the future of our world.
We cannot go back.
I cannot give my childhood to my heirs;
Maybe they would not want it,
But can we save some treasures to enrich their life?
Can the wild poppies and the butterflies survive?
Can the exotic forest-dwellers cheat extinction?
Can we do this?
Or it is now too late?

A Josephine Allen

FIRST LOVE

I remember back to that first day,
When we met each other, I couldn't say,
How happy I felt with you by my side,
We lived in a paradise, and our dreams were wild,
Our moments were precious and full of love,
We thought 'twould last forever,
O heavens above.

The times we spent strolling around,
Arm in arm we felt so proud.
The simple things we loved to do,
Like walks in the park, or playing pool,
They all meant so much to me and you.
We lived for the weekends, when we could be alone,
And nothing else mattered, the world was our own.

But that's in the past, and time moves on,
It was our first love, like a beautiful song.
But though we've gone our separate ways,
I'll always have memories of those happy days.
And looking back, I'm sure you'll agree,
It was a wonderful time, for you and me.

Tommy Devine

THE LIFETIME OF MY DISCONTENT

I want to see the sun from where I stand and watch it sink away
I want to lose myself between the trees and mould myself in clay
For I cannot relate to many things which were once a part of me
Because I am not the king I thought I was but half the man I used to be

I want the day to die along with the night and my body to lose its mind
I want to see the stars fall from the sky and in an instant strike me blind
I would like to know what it would be like to feel it from the inside
But that I suppose no-one really knows for they have lost their minds

I want to steal my flowers from everyone and watch them die just for fun
I want to buy my friend a little hat and a little badge so they may match
his gun
I want to count pebbles on the shore to send to my friend who is no more
But they are too heavy so I will leave them there, leave them there beside
the door

I want to see the sun from the door where I stand and watch it sink away
I want to leave the trees and all the leaves and break my mould of clay
For I relate too much to things which are nothing to do with me
Because I am not the king I thought I was but half the man I used to be

Niall Farrell

MY GRIEVING THOUGHTS

The day she went to heaven I know it had to be
She didn't go by herself she took a part of me.
God only gives one mother He only gives one chance
This pain I have to carry is piercing like a lance.

When she went away I only thought of me
Where did she go? If only I could see.
My mind was so confused it just would not clear
I didn't have the sense to know that she would always be near.

My heart is broke in two the wound is open wide
But I know I will survive for God is on my side
When I am all alone I softly call her name
My life has changed so much it will never be the same.

But I know she's happy as happy as can be
I miss her very much and wonder does she miss me.
I didn't say goodbye I didn't hold her hand
I could only pray to God that she would understand.

From ever I remember I dreaded the day
When God would call her name and ask her to stay.
I know she is safe in her haven in the sky
I think it is time I stopped asking why?

I thank God for what I have and also what I had
I don't mean to be ungrateful but you see God, I still am sad.
Better to have loved and lost than never loved at all
But someday we'll meet again when you decide to call.

Mary Loughery

OF USE NO MORE

Crow, spread-eagled on the Hawthorne,
Grabbed in mid-flight
As it beat its miserable retreat
Across Northern fields.

The wind sounded its Tocsin warning,
And all the elements set to work
On the creature's miserable body.

There is no escape from here!
Your murderous shadow extinguished -
Your *ca-w* cry a painful and
Unforgettable memory of the past,
And the Starry Plough once more
Will light the way.

Bill Webster

SUN

Dawn erupted with a brilliant streak of light,
That danced joyously in reflection, to chase away the night.
The bright white sun enveloped the horizon,
Illuminating yet smothering, that star I had my eyes on.

That golden shadow brings warmth and nourishment to the land,
Like the love that breathes life to the wedding band,
We should pay homage to that which is more powerful than man,
For without him I fear we never can.

Carl Olsen

SOLITUDE

I remember a curlew calling
A lonesome plaintive cry,
And the dark Donegal hills
Reaching up clawing the rain from the sky,
The river racing north, brown and swollen
Bearing seaward man's discarded waste,
The long slender reeds gyrating madly
Before the onslaught of the driving rain
Like dancers in a frenzied dance.
There was a kind of peace and solitude
On that rain swept river bank,
I was oblivious of the wet clothing
Clinging to my body, or the world beyond.
I walked alone a minute part of that time.

Alexander Sandy Jack

WHAT NEXT?

Hail to the new millennium!
Awaited by some with pleasure.
Others fear the end is near,
they do not seek for treasure.
Sperm count down? No future here
for those free-learning nursery vouchers.
Young teachers eagerly plying their trade
may end up living as slouchers.
Hail to the new millennium!
By great monuments, cheers and celebrations,
credit card highs - no-effort buys,
plastic swells the currency of nations.
If leisure reigns over the wise,
was there a task like 'work'?
We blessed this four-letter friend,
others swear it drives them beserk.
Hail to the new millennium!
Knowledge has taken a downward trend.
Maybe there ought to be clowns
in the wings ready to send
lightness of heart - lifting the frowns.
Giving loud voice to the text,
with unopened ears - eyes missing code,
all prayers are said - what next?
Hail to the new millennium!

Lena Cooper

GARVAGHY PRIMARY SCHOOL, CO DOWN

The little building shivers in the twilight
The late sun's rays could not her heat restore.
An era ends as the iron key turns slowly
And no more children's laughter round her door.

Another day will dawn, but not for her now,
Her job's completed and her education done.
A century or more she's watched her children
But now her life ebbs with the setting sun.

Grandfathers, fathers, sons have passed her threshold,
She's guarded them as they learned good from ill,
She's watched their lives from childhood through to adult
Like a sentinel upon Garvaghy hill.

Many years I entered through her portals,
In snowy winter, glad to be inside
Around the glowing stove and then, in summer
When joyfully she'd fling her windows wide.

Is this to be her fate now, lone and silent,
Soft skipping songs and sums no more she'll share.
Two-classroom schools are finished, say the experts
As chalk dust settles on her floorboards bare.

But wait! She shivers, shaking off her musings,
The parish church accepts her back again
For Sunday School and harvest teas she's suited
A grand church hall she will become for them.

Parish events now happen 'neath her rafters.
Once more she fills with happy laughter shrill.
She stretches, smiles and looks towards the future -
That little school upon Garvaghy Hill.

Alma Ferguson

HAWTHORN DAYS

O, the sweet, sweet honey scent
Of the hawthorn flower,
The snow flower lying
Softly asleep
Upon the emerald fire
Of green hedges, and hawthorn tree.

When I was young
And far away from my own land -
I might have been content
With Mediterranean blue sea
And burning sky,
I might have been enchanted
With the vines so rich
Upon the red earth of the hills,
Or soft green of olive trees.

Yet upon a far mysterious
Mist of time,
Came the old twisted form
Of a hawthorn tree,
And upon a cool clear air
Came this wild sweet scent
Overpowering all the senses
And calling me home.

Jean Mary Orr

TWO SECONDS TO THE MIDNIGHT EXPRESS

At the climax of Giro day, I push Mr Salvation away,
Kick his 'I can save you' tambourine to his washed lily hands,
Then enter the welcome to hell doors of Old Mulligans bar.
The familiar stench blends well with its bastard clientele and
The instant Mr Jameson and I touch it's a silken symbiosis,
for his glass eye vision blurs my world.

Passing out towards the floor a tweed jacket wrapped round a Heineken belly
acts as my cushion,
Shortly the copulation of fist on cheek gives birth to a swollen eye
and on the street across
A beggar's ballad bellows from a broken window that masquerades
as a poor man's megaphone for a merciless world.
Stumbling down the lane the whiskey sodden abacus in my head counts every
unfamiliar breath,
For the next world is a doorway, a swift hand and a greeting from Sheffield's
finest away.

My face is now lit by one godless light in the night sky, shining on my sweet
jungle town,
Protect and serve cop sirens scatter soulless shadows from the ghost streets
below.
Drunken by St Christopher's bridge, I catch the roar of the midnight express,
In Rumple-Mintz inspired dreams she speeds like ice in my veins and carries
me to Holly wood.

Polluted rain hits my face as I crawl up my steps,
it cascades to my lips and is an appetiser for the future shock to come.
In the confines of my bedsit my wall mirror is companionship through
insomnia nights,
Miss Hunger is her comrade and they mingle till the new dawn tries to
resurrect life.

In the darkest terminal days Miss Needle eclipses Senorita Mary-Jane as my sweetheart,
After the thrill of making love she leaves,
Someday soon we'll both leave forever.

Stephen Fisher

THE VISION

I get a glimpse
But oh so small
Again, again
Yet that is all.

Nothing more
Nothing less
But just enough
For me to guess
The beauty and the calm there is
The love for everyone.

Each breath a caress
Each sigh
A sigh of peace.
For although it's there
I cannot see,
Although it's near
I cannot feel.

And as the door shuts,
Coldness returns.
The cries of the needy,
The grunts of the greedy.
And I shiver.
I cry.
But know that I am loved
Know that you are there.

Sinead Cox

LONELINESS

Green filtered light
A napkin bright
A damp tissue
- A café I remember.

Where loneliness is middle-aged
and seated in slacks
Is sipping cold coffee alone
With shadow circles
And turned backs.

And a sudden loss of control
Is a breakdown
A grief display - a let-down.

And everywhere - embarrassment
Is not wanting to look
But compelled to stare
At red-blotched face disgrace.

Whether music is a happy memory recall
For a forever lost never found
Moment?

Or couple secluded young love
Is vivid, bright and too much
For middle-aged regret?

Is a permanent despair.

A few moments of visible upset
was all she gave -
Then - the tissue and the bill paid.

And loneliness
Is an empty chair
in a café I remember.

Helen Fallows

MEMORY LANE

A time to ponder in my brain
When I would walk down memory lane
Remember days of old, the mates I had
The stories told.
The roads so broad, the walls so high
They seem to reach up to the sky
For we were small the days so long,
The summertime would march along.
And I would wonder of days to come,
Now they are here I don't sing that song,
I like you let them march along.
The lane no longer stands on ground,
Where feet marched and churned around.
The legs so strong, the years to grow.
I am tired it's time to go
The mind willing the body weak,
It's time for me to have that sleep,
Another day has yet to come when me and mates,
Will soldier on, I know not where they are today
But with God's help we will meet some day.

James Frew

A POEM ABOUT AN ESTATE AGENT

By most standards
An impressive home.
Go on, get a loan.
Look outside
Behind the shed,
There's a nice wee spot
To bury the dead.

Ian G

INNER CHILD

Awaken, little girl
You are not extinct.
Activate your untainted innocence
And we will consolidate.

Run carefree in the sand
Feeling the grit olive-brown dust
Sinking into its shimmery complexion.

Smile at the sun,
Your ruling planet.
Derive your energy from this radiant source.

Splash in the sea, screaming excitedly.
Flying masses of liquid
Conspiring with laughter,
Stirring you to activity
And seducing your elation.

Come, little girl
And I will receive you.
Each breath you inhale
Unite with mine.
Exhaling together we'll reach our divinity,
Female deities
Of beauty and grace.

Caroline Gallagher

ANISEED BALLS AND NOUGAT

Memories are peculiar things,
they offer only snatches and glimpses
never the whole.
When I remember my Granda
I remember he was tall with big gentle hands.
I remember Saturday walks to the local Saturday morning league;
McCafferty's shop where he bought me sweets,
Aniseed Balls and Nougat.
I can remember the woody, aromatic smell of his pipe,
the huge black spits he let fly
on the ground as he munched his tobacco.
But I can't remember his illness.
'He only lay a few weeks.'
As me and my brothers played Cowboys and Indians
feigning death by bullet and arrow,
Granda passed silently away.
And I was too young to be allowed to say goodbye.

Bernadette McFadden

BOXING DAY WALK 1995

Winter white, sharp and crisp
A walk on ice roads
Not to be missed!
See the boughs standing
Majestic and clean
Not a movement or ripple,
No motion is seen.

Icicles hang from an old tin spout
I want to break one off, and shout!
For stillness, is all around us now,
I know I'll echo, and yet somehow
I resist the urge, I look in awe,
At the patterns of frost on the frozen haw.
Spiders cobwebs, fragile glass,
Caught for today, but today will pass.

I watch my breath, vanish, go
I love this season, I love the snow!
Sharp, crisp frost, gives a new dimension
This is our creators, own invention!
How long has it been, since we thanked
Him for
All that he sends? Even frozen haw!

Mary McCullough

M

Tonight our souls touched over the ocean,
As we danced for hours on the stratosphere.
We sat together in the theatre of the clouds
And sang the symphony of the gulls.
Afterwards,
when the moon had run its race,
We descended softly to the earth,
and with a gentle kiss,
we parted.

Humphrey Dunn

THE BANN VALLEY

There's a quiet and beautiful valley
All made from a river and lee;
From Lough Beg through the bridges and meadows
To where it flows into the sea.

No artist could paint such a picture
Or poet pen such a song;
To see or to hear its adventures
While it makes its still journey along.

The cattle enjoy its refreshments
By its banks as they leisurely stray.
The birds warble sweet on the hedgerows
When it comes to the close of the day.

There are stretches of forest and foliage
Where the foxes can hide in their dens
There are bluebells and sweet scented flowers
Round the curves, the slopes and the bends.

Along the fair county of Derry
With the heather in bloom by its side;
The bees humming gay in the sunshine
Gathering honey with pride.

The swans with their snowy white pinions
Love to swim in the water so clear.
They hatch out their young by its borders
When it comes to their time of the year.

When you stand on the high hills of Antrim
And gaze on this valley so grand
Can you think on the one who arranged it
The work of the Lord's mighty hand.

Nellie Bell

THE HARVEST

As I look across the countryside
So different every day
Today the beauty that I see
My breath it takes away
The sun is shining on the fields
Gold and green all around
The shadows of the trees are there
The shadows they are long
The trees are changing colour
I stand and look in awe

And there below the trees
The cows they stand around
The summer sun has left
Little grass upon the ground
The sheep they graze
No grass can be found
But still all day they run and play
Around the hedges at night they stay

It's night-time now as I look out
No colour all around
And there in the sky the harvest moon
The brightest to be found
It brightens up the countryside
The trees they look so different
The cows and sheep are fast asleep
It's time for me the stairs to creep

Nan Kelly

COURTING IN THE KITCHEN

I heard the bombs blast
Carried close on the water.
Kissed you, held you tighter,
talked and laughed.
Let you love me,
as you should
for I loved you.

That's courting in the kitchen
the only thing I ever knew

Then, walking home I watched
the half moon glow
behind the halo
of the street lamp.
Thought of you,
felt God somewhere near.

I watched a man stand
in the shadow of the phone box. Hands
cradling his head.
Eyes shining close to tears.
And the young tree
lying broken on the field.
Torn from the earth
But not yet dead.

Liam McLaughlin

FIRE

What is the fascination of a fire?
Coal fire, turf fire, timber fire.
To sit round a fire, listen as the
Gases hiss and another ember rises.
No-one speaks, all are caught in the
Hypnotic trance of the fire. As the
Wind rises and the windows rattle and
Midnight comes, somebody suggests telling
A ghost story. Already the fire is casting
Shadows, and one casts cautious looks over
One's shoulder, and we draw nearer to the
Comfort of the fire, as our ancestors did
In the primeval cave.
But now-a-days we have central heating and
Other means of heating our homes, and on
Stormy nights our windows don't rattle, and
Central heating does not cast shadows, or
Embers that rise and fall, no hissing gases.
Beautiful colours, no-one tells ghost stories,
And we don't cast cautious looks over our shoulders,
We watch Hammer movies on television!

Gerry Kenny

REFLECTIONS

Sleep sweet children
Close thine eyes
Far above you starry skies
Angels on silent wings do fly
Protect and guard you
While you lie.

Rest beside me
Mother dear
Soon the dawning will appear
Then your troubles
Will be gone
Disappearing with the morn.

Stumble not my love
Nor cry
Draw thy breath
Love's sweet sigh
Feel the sun upon thy brow
Fear not death as it draws nigh.

O my loves I see thee now
As I sit and close my eyes
Hear thy laughter
See thy tears
Memories of yesteryears
Now though old and frail I be
In my heart I carry thee.

Kim Kilpatrick

THE PAINT-BOX

(A poem for Northern Ireland)

I had a paint-box.
But it didn't have the colour red
For the anger and the bloodshed,
Nor white
For the hearts and faces of our dead.
It didn't have silver
For the tears that could flood
A thousand loughs,
Or black
For the shadows of the gunmen.

Instead, it had orange
For the rising and setting of the sun
And pink
For the hopes and dreams of our people.
There was green
For the fertility of our land
And yellow
For the smiles of our children.
I had a paint-box,
So I painted peace.

Kathryn Forde

A SIGN OF SPRING

Across this land
From farm to farm
No happier sight
Will be seen

Than those playful lambs
As around their dams
Do fondly sport and play

This sight of spring
To us all does bring
A sign of hope and cheer

For those summer months
When we too, will know
And be able to show
A little spring in our heel.

Sam Dunbar

DO ANGELS HAVE WINGS?

Do angels have wings? -
Can an elephant fly?
Is the ocean red?
Or the sea, the sky?

Perhaps in a world of make-believe
Or a cartoon strip on comic land
Perhaps in a world beyond the sky,
But what about wings in the here and now?

I know of some angels, so caring and kind,
Who do not wear haloes or have wings fixed behind,
But angels they are, though quite unaware,
To all of the patients who are under their care.
These angels wear yellow,
While others bear blue,
And some clad in green, or in navy too.

If you really feel ill, you've only to say,
And they'll fetch up your meals
On a hospital tray.

If you're feeling dizzy,
Or have 'wobbly' knees,
They'll come to your aid,
With a fresh cup of tea.

Their vigil they keep by day and by night,
Ensuring their flock are keeping all right.
And if you can't settle yourself for a sleep,
A cup of hot milk will bring relief.
But if that doesn't work as it usually will,
They will ring up the 'Doc' for a new sleeping pill.

Evans Hunniford

FERGUSON MASSEY

At our library proudly stands
The statue of a man
Who brought pride to this land
He left the shores of Ireland
To reach the hearts of others
Well, he made it to the top
Yes, Limavady proudly presents
A former Australian Prime Minister
His name Ferguson Massey.

Orinda Bellingham

STOOD UP!

Meaningful, meaningless
What does it mean?
Anyone can guess.
Perhaps it was meant
When it was said,
What does it mean
In your head?

Meaningful, meaningless
What's in a word?
Anyone can guess.
The only contract
Is a rope or a chain,
What's in a word
When you're waiting in the rain?

Sonya Cotton

MOTHER

A mother is a special person
unique in every way
her love never fades or weakens
it just gets stronger day by day.

In times of joy or sorrow
she'll be there to help you through,
a mother's love is there for you
no matter what you do.

If you cry she will cry with you,
if you laugh she'll do that too;
because a mother's love is precious
and sincere through and through.

The love you give me Mummy
is more special than the rest
I'm proud to be your daughter
and as a mother *'You're the best'*.

Tracy Branagan

MY ANIMAL FRIENDS

I love to sit in the meadow
When the sun is shining bright,
Admiring the buttercups and daisies.
Oh! 'What a lovely sight.'

The hens they noisily cackle,
The ducks are noisy too,
And the fluffy little chickens,
Keep pecking at the dew.

The kittens come and peep at them.
They wonder what they are.
The mother hen starts clucking,
And nearly starts a war.

Soon all is quiet and peaceful.
Just a kitten's faint mew,
When suddenly the peace is shattered.
By *Cock-a-doodle-doo!*

He is standing on a haystack,
Looking, oh so proud,
His feathers like the rainbow,
And his call so clear and loud.

It's Sir Jeffrey my handsome rooster,
He is the leader of them all.
The hens all come running,
In answer to his call.

Jean Monteith

THE BIRTHDAY BROOCH

Rowing my love to Fishloughan Island
A little way up the calm River Bann,
At last we're truly alone together
Out in this beautiful August weather.

Where trees lie resting upon the water
Stirred but briefly by our flirty laughter,
As on I row with a hastening heart
Hoping our excursion will light love's spark.

And arriving at our destination
I can sense a great anticipation,
As safe in my arms I help her ashore
To enjoy the picnic we came here for.

A bottle of bubbly, and some good food,
And off we step through the island's dense wood.
She is everything I'm thinking of,
As I wander deeper into her love.

But what could this be, shining in the grass?
My curiosity won't let me pass.
On kneeling down, it looks familiar,
Could it be the birthday brooch I gave her?

'I think you'd better take me home' she says,
And her sentence shatters my happiness;
I thought she'd grown much more than a friend,
But now our friendship has come to an end.

Piqued, I throw the brooch into the river,
It's gone forever, but I still love her;
Yet, the waters of time may wash away,
The pain of rejection I feel today.

Paul Hutton

SILENCE

As each day dawns
I hear birds sing
But a silence rings louder
In my lonely room
Then down the stairs
Each step I take
Wishing, hoping
But always no.
Not a sound of the friendly whistle
Or tapping computer
In the room below,
I call his name
No answer back.
My dear one's gone
So many words left unspoken
Too late
This silence can't be broken.

Norma McCullough

I

If only I had known then, the treasures life has shown me
I could have changed the things I'd done, the failures I now see,
Those many little miracles, I so mistook for chance
The very fact that I'm alive, taken for granted at a glance.

One hundred million receptors, placed within one eye
The uniqueness of a starlit night, a canvas in the sky
Twenty-four thousand fibres, placed within one ear
The singing of a nightingale, that gift that we call 'hear'.

Seven miles of nerve fibre, synchronised to do your will
Thirty-six million beats a year, from a heart that never stills
Thirteen billion nerve cells, within the three-pound brain
To feel, touch, taste and smell, how can we complain?

From our Father in supreme love, came from four hundred million choices
Four hundred million pairs of eyes, ears and legs and voices
Searching for the other half, they all gave up and died
You're the one who won that race, gaining rights to grow inside.

Protected in your mother's womb, till growing time was through
What happened was a miracle, the miracle was *you*
We were not made at a careless whim, in the laboratory of life
We're a manifestation of God-given love, a creation of 'husband and wife'.

You cannot improve on a miracle, accept it for how it will be
When you look in the mirror, the reflection that's there, is the 'one off'
                                        of you and of me
When I look at the things that are beautiful, the things that never shall die
I'll never be worthless, never be nothing, I'm someone, and something, I'm
I.

Look forward to today, not tomorrow, leave regrets and mistakes to the past
We only have now, it's here to be lived, you're the playwright; the world
                                        is your cast!

Brenda McCrossan

CAVERN OF JOY

Searching in silence with eyes that listen
The prodigal daughter returns with a mission

With a mantle of hope she went to her Father
The puzzle of her life found ineffable rapture

An iridescent future now abounds with a burning zeal
Illuminated by a timeless eternity with a heavenly seal

The husk of her soul is jewelled with a secret love
For she has managed to escape life's perils by his blood.

Pauline Holmes

HUNTED

The fox stole out on silent sleepless sunset
To hunt down leafy lanes in weary hours,
Cubs hanging on the precipice of hunger
Lay sheltered 'neath the earth from night-time showers.

Along low hedgerows the creeping crimson stalked
To fix her eyes on unsuspecting quarry,
In vice-like teeth the lifeless victim lay
And then to starving offspring home would carry.

This night as dark draws close to dawn
The hunter crosses field to stand by tarmac's edge,
That long dark line of man-made quarried stone
Lies still between two rows of planted hedge.

Down road comes sound of mechanical combustion
And two strong beams of brightness shone,
See fox terrified, frozen, dazzled,
In one brief passing instant life is gone.

The tracker's wile no match for charging metal,
No more the vixen searches near or far
Just bruised and broken breathless body,
Nature's cunning hunter, hunted by the car.

King Anderson

GROWING OLD

It's hard to cope with growing old
Each day could be our last
It's hard to cope with loneliness
And dwelling on the past

But don't look back with bitterness
For all the things you didn't do
Just say, Thank God I'm still alive
Although you're feeling blue

If you can walk, and you can talk
And you can also see
You are one of the lucky ones
Not crippled and blind like me

So face the world with a great big smile
Forget you're old - stay young for a while
For life is what you make it, I'm sure you will agree
Although I can't walk, although I can't talk,
The smile that you see is from me.

Mary Devine

A LOSING BATTLE

Where do they come from?
Those little white things,
That hide in the atmosphere,
Hover, then spring! And land
On that part of the rug
You've just done - and
Lie there, resplendent,
Like pearls in the sun.
Defiant, triumphant!
They've foiled you again -
That zeal you once had
Is beginning to wane.
No matter how often
You charge with your vac,
Those white faery temptresses
Keep coming back!

Mary P Sweeney

WHO?

Who? Will take my hand
when my steps are weak;
and reply for me when I cannot speak

Who? Will listen for me
when I cannot hear;
lighten up my heart and calm my dreadful fear

Who? Will see for me
when my eyes are dim;
say a prayer for me as I pray to Him

Who? Will comfort me
through my cares and woes;
help me keep my sanity when my reason goes

Who? Will cheer me
when I'm tired of life;
no-one but my dearest dear - my true and loving wife

Matthew Cosby

SICK

Sat on the sill
As close as I can
Get to the heat and the legs
And the heels of the fecund
And the well.

Window mists up
With the heat
I suck from them
Heaving eyes blinded.
Drowned by my own breath.

Joel Smith

HOME TOWN

There is a town down in Tyrone
That I will always call my own
It's been many years since from there I went
My happiest days were around there spent
Fun-filled days 'neath the summer sun
In the golden days when I was young.

Come walk along the road with me
Back through five and fifty years
Share again with me those carefree days
When there was little pain or tears
In the warm care of kith and kin
Around that friendly town 'Drumquin'.

The old Main Street is much the same
Tho' many a shop has changed its name
Slowly still does the river flow
As in the days so long ago
When to the school house now laid low
In noisy groups we all did go.

Wander over the old back road
Beneath the setting sun.
Along this way to the crooked bridge
We used to have such fun
Coming from the dances in the hall
In the days when I was young.

In the noisy city far away
My thoughts will turn at the close of day
Back to that town down in Tyrone
That I will always call my own
And listen again as Kemoney's song is sung
About the hills above Drumquin.

Gerry Skelton

THE REALM OF ROSES

Absence from our souls,
Escapism from our minds,
The only way to survive,
Losing one so close, yet now out of reach.

Then we can,
Cross impossible seas together,
Deny disaster its victory over us,
Resist the elevated fall.

Stop indicating our own deficiencies
Underestimating our talents,
Yield up our hopes to save,
The need for battle.

Battled love is all that is true,
Something that cannot be taken
Only enviably given.

We talk instead of merely communicating.
About the death of stubborn pride
For it has no place in love,
As love and pride keep no company
In the realm of roses.

Liam Quigley

A DIFFERENT WORLD

She looks like any other this child who filled my life,
We waited many years to have this precious girl of light.
Hair that's curled and golden, eyes of emerald green,
But in their depths, if you look close, a different world is seen.
Her smile can fill the darkest place with sunshine and with flowers,
This very special child of mine who stares for hours and hours.
She has no voice to shout and scream, not threats and no demands,
Yet for her I'd give my all to see her scheme and plan,
A future like the others', make-up, clothes and boys,
This special girl will never know what we call our life's joys.
I wonder when I look at her and see her ease and grace, is
There somewhere that she resides 'tween heaven, here, and space?
Have any one of us this look of true contented heart?
She'll never gossip, hurt or wound, from that she stands apart.
Yes . . . this child is special, for all the world to see,
She fills our home with her own light, as close to God can be.
Is there a place for angels in this world of super powers?
'Cause I am sure that one lives here in this small home of ours.

Evelyn Peoples

CWP

Hail to the Celtic Warrior Poets
Hail to them and their glorious deeds
To their gallant spirit from ages past
Aptly conveyed to their contemporary seed.

Those simple men of timeless esteem
Who charged the fields of battle in defence of simple needs.
Humble men endowed with immortal honour
Making us who we are and proud to call them kin.

Our birthright calls us to exemplify such noble nature
To portray a warrior's courage and a poet's soul
A task our hearts are joyous and proud to engage
As we would rather be seen as men in the eyes
Of the CWP than kings in any others.

Caoimhin O'Hannrachtaigh

DUAL GAP

Few see it, lucky not to.
Long term pain, he moves towards it
Darkness ahead and then a door.
Once locked, chains lie around it broken
An open door and light ahead.
Moving out, a chain still holds him
Never truly lets him go.
More milligrams, they draw him forward
A miracle, such difference;
No.

Shaking starts, the others notice
Speech impaired, the others hear.
Fight to save him
Flailing, failing science.
Arms stretched ahead, the chain is pulling
Pulling back towards the door.
Gathers speed, the others follow
Dropping back, the grip is lost.
A barrier, cannot go on.
It slams.
Chains lifting, sweeping
Expression gone, emotion stifled.
Lost in darkness, calling, screaming
A spirit thriving, no language heard.
Merely sensed, yearned for
By those who love him only.

Chris McLaughlin

THE INNOCENCE OF BEAUTY

A life of simple pleasures in her world of make believe
The summer sun shines bright naked she sleeps in the cool of the night
Spends her hours out walking or swimming in the river
Dreams of a knight in shining armour and a passionate love that burns
                                                                inside her
This is an innocence untainted seen through the searching eyes of a child
Growing into womanhood tangled emotions running wild
Lost in a world of romance where the roses never fade
Knowing each other's thoughts when not a word was said
Believes in all the magic wishes on every star
Everything is beautiful and beauty is what you are

Robert J McManus

WHITE SNOW-CAPS

Mountain tops with white snow-caps
Patchwork quilt of green
Spread along with scalloped edge
Co-ordinating all those shades of green

What a picture to gaze upon
Mountains fall and rise
Mountain tops with white snow-caps
Silhouetted against the sky

Gazing upon this picturesque scene
Colours blending through
Spring's bright sunshine rays
A golden spectacular hue
Rooks fly, hurrying by
Flapping to elm trees on high

Pussy willows toss in harmony
Disturbed by chilling breeze
Springtime's chilling winds lingering
Perhaps the last harsh breath
Waving goodbye, goodbye
To mountain tops with white snow-caps
Silhouetted against the sky
To the snow of spring
Rooks on the wing caw caw goodbye

Frances Gibson

THE BEAUTIFUL WOMEN
(Thoughts in a Residential Home for the Elderly)

Beneath are the beautiful women
Who are drifting along with the tide,
Their bodies are changing around them
Though they are still lovely inside.

They rejoiced in their homes and their families,
Bought gifts to arrange round the tree,
Loved perfumes and stains and laces
And having their hair done 'at three'.

They loved shopping for hats, in the spring-time
And birthdays and dinners and wine
The making of jam and the sewing,
And washing that blew on the line.

There were picnics and trips to the country
And taking the kids to the sea
And trying to keep up with the fashion,
And having their friends in for tea.

So I weep for the beautiful women
As they silently sit in a row,
And I sigh for the years that are passing
And the days that are melting like snow.

As we care for the beautiful women
With cheeks now all wrinkled and drawn,
Do they smile as they doze and remember
The sweetness of days that are gone?

Rosemary Williamson

HER VOICE

She is calling to me from a distance
She knows I can sense she is there
The sound of her voice fills my being
I stop what I'm doing and stare . . .
Out over green fields and horizons
To the clouds and the blue skies above
My eyes misting over with longing
For the mother who reared me with love.

But she could not be here, my dear mother
Far off lands keep her miles, miles away
But I do hear her voice . . . no mistaking
I must go home now . . . yes, today!

I am walking the lane to the farmyard
Her voice ringing clear in my ears
My steps getting faster, now lengthen
But why am I weeping hot tears?
The lane is so long . . . I'd forgotten!
I hear voices, see some folks by the gate
They look round, bow their heads and stay silent
I know then that I've come home too late.

She was calling to me from a distance
She knew I would sense she was there
That voice, now silenced, still echoes
As it drifts back to me on the air.

D J Farrell

CHRYSALIS

(On the release of Jackie Mann, Beirut hostage, September 1991)

Fragile
Gentlemanly
Aged victim
Vaulted
In darkness
Silence
Heat.
Mummified alive.

Capture doffed
To reveal
A resilience
A smile
A graciousness
An eloquence
A spirit transcending
The height of the planes he once flew.

Valerie McCausland

THROUGH OUR IRISH EYES

They see a gun in place of a shamrock,
They see a murder in place of a smile,
No-one can see the beauty which we see,
The splendour seen only through our Irish eyes.

They see a killer in place of a farmer,
They see a victim in place of a child,
They do not see past the news and the papers,
Things which are seen only by our Irish eyes.

Perhaps one day they will see us as we see,
The beauty of Antrim and Armagh and Down,
The history of Derry and beauty within it,
The charm which exists in my lovely home town.

Joanne Harkens

NATURE'S NEWSPAPER

I do not need the newspaper, radio or TV
The news items are in nature, plain to see.

Murder
Last night the big brown fox sneaked out,
Today, the cock-pheasant is no longer about.

Robbery
Those greedy rooks have carried away and ate
The pale blue eggs from the nest at the gate.

Disaster
The gale force winds blew down the apple tree,
No more home for the pigeons three.

Birth
From a clever chrysalis below the sill nearby,
A butterfly emerged and soared into the sky.

Marriage
The yellow-billed blackbird looks so pleased,
His wife has finished their nest with ease.

Fight
Two robins red both liked the site,
But one of them was put to flight.

Why every topic in the news,
Nature has it . . . just choose.

R G Harkness

THE FATHER TESTING

There was an air of excitement,
As my dad called me -
'C'mon son, we have to catch
Them there horses at the hill for shawing.'

It was about two miles to the hill,
Part by road, part through field
And wasteland.

My little legs could just about keep up
As my dad strode on
With power and grace
He reminded me of the horses in a way.

As we neared the horses
I felt those awful butterflies in my stomach
For I knew this time
He would give me the leading rope.

The horses were huge and powerful
But beautiful - and not fully tamed.

I was scared, but did not tell dad
For I wanted him to be proud of me
And tell everyone in the pub that night.

Dad caught one and called me over
He handed me the rope
And let go himself
I smiled at him and made a clicking sound
To make the horse walk.

At that he stopped me
And took the rope off me saying
'Ye'll have to wait a year or two yet,
I just wanted to see if ye had it in ye.'

Rayner Irwin

SUMMER TIME

I sat beside a valley stream
On a warm and sunny day
The silver perch were springing high
As they glided on their way
The cowslip and buttercup
Edged the mossy bank
And the cuckoo and the curlew sang
Like music heard in dreams.

The sky it was an azure blue
With an odd white cloud in sight
The temperatures were soaring high
The swallow high in flight
The distant shouts of children
Broke the tranquil silence there
The water babbling o'er the stones
Just made you sit and stare.

The lush green pastures stretching out
Like a lovely patchwork quilt.
The little lambs were bleating
And frisking all about.
The chestnuts and the elms
Stood reaching to the skies
While the magpie and the blackbird
Kept a staring watchful eye, for all the
Crusts I threw to them
As I ate my bit of lunch.

Mary Cartmill

IN MEMORY OF A FLAME
(In memory of Catherine Benson)

Is life a mere candle?
The comparison is made that we are but dim lights
which in nigh time must fade.
And too often we look at the smoke in the rain
and wonder where we would be
if the flame were still burning bright
with the light we once knew,
and we hammer at why things must pass as they do.

And yet we are thankful
For all the years when the flame lit our hearts
with its laughter and tears.
For the way that it danced and brought warmth to our day
With its carefree tangle of colours at play.
A circle of light that pooled with our own
Flickering in joy or acting the clown
Humming its tune with a smile as it shone
Brightening our lives
Though now it is gone
And we suffer the sorrow of yesterday's flame
Unlit for tomorrow.

Yet our Father above will cry too for our pain
On this same old earth he once too lost a flame.
So we pray that in time our flames will unite
once again,
and forever,
together in light.

Sue Gallagher

UNTIMELY

When we knew we were wide-eyed,
Numb,
Silently screaming,
Wanting to pick you up
And run.
But there was nowhere to run,
No hiding place for us
Or you beneath the naked sun.
Now we whimper
In the scorching baldness
Of reality,
Longing for shadows.

Ann Stewart

DOWN BY FAUGHAN SIDE

(A tribute to Olly McGilloway)

Describing the woods in words
dense as deep water;
your face as contoured
as the crags you craved.
Bushy-browed,
sluicing through hills;
belonging as brontosaurus.

Over Lough Swilly, to Bloody Foreland
or the islets below Fanad,
you heaved; to herald a heron;
paved praisings for snipe or shrew.
Bothering with beasts and birds
that our love never knew.

Striding strew speedwell or saladine,
delphinius or dewdrop.
Lost in the land like a leaf
from a souled tree;

Lord of the Lily,
Galahad of glen,
May your wand weave,
away from men.

Seán Cribben

HOME TRUTHS

If I don't speak,
you won't have to
listen.

Safe in my silence,
you'll never need fear
any danger from
knowing.

Worlds beyond your borders
rotate around suns
different - and yet similar -
to your own.

No need to worry.
You won't be blinded
by anyone's brilliance
but your own;

and you are bright,
you know.
Bright as the hell
you talk so much about
and condemn so many to.

No, don't worry.
I won't speak
what you won't hear;

secure in your Truth,
you'll never need know
how much is unknowable,
and true,
beyond the borders of salvation.

Julie Craig

SILENT PLACES

Why do I seek for silent places
Where I can be alone with my maker
And ponder in my mind wonders and
   thoughts?

Why do I seek for silent places
With darkness and quiet
And a single ray of light
Which is invisible in the sun
But seems so bright in this silent place
Warming my skin
The touch of my maker?

Why do I seek for silent places
Where I see the wonders of the universe
And think the thoughts of God?
The silence speaks the words of God
Like whispers in my head
And I see the glory of God in the
   darkness above.

P Knipe

MY HOMETOWN

Banbridge town in the County Down
is where my heart will always be.
I left it many years ago
but from my mind it will not go.
I love the people and their ways
And though I'm not too far away
I yearn for home almost every day.
Memories came back to me
When I return to the Bann and see
the people and places I love so well.

The hole in the middle they call 'the Cut'
has filled my mind with 'ifs' and 'buts'.
If it were not there who would really care?
But then I sit and think a while
And upon my face there comes a smile.
I would care if it were not there
Because from the town would go the heart
Beside 'the Cut' the 'Welcome' is
Where memories are shared and friendships start.
All in all it's a grand wee town
My own little corner of County Down.

Colette Brown

THE SANDWICH

It sits there silently
Dripping mayonnaise onto the patterned plate
Lettuce droops - cucumber and tomatoes sit still
Waiting - watching
From inside peeps a slice of cheese -
Thick yellow and inviting!

I look at it
My lips trembling every second
I try to think of something else -
It calls to me!

Finally, I sit up
I can bear it no longer
I pick up the wholemeal sandwich
It drops on the floor, I mop it up!

Sarah Walsh (12)

CREATIVE THOUGHT

At his workbench he laboured,
days, weeks, months, by day and night;
he chiselled, planed, sandpapered,
but he couldn't get it right.
Calmly he cast it aside,
and with careful selection,
yet another piece he tried,
still working for perfection.
Then one early afternoon
he stopped, weary and saddened.
He expected something soon:
he waited,
nothing happened.
Sitting down he wiped his brow:
'One last time, just one last time,
for I cannot give up now,
I'll finish this work of mine.'
He stood up. Again he worked
days, weeks, months, with little rest.
Flaws he saw, but overlooked.
Then he stared like one obsessed,
his face no longer saddened,
no doubts now, but believing.
And suddenly it happened.
She started gently breathing -
his vision was coming true.
Standing back, his hands on hips,
she opened her eyes of blue
and she moved her lovely lips.
And when she had turned her head,
with some emotion:
'My finest creation yet!' he said.

Robert E Corrigan

PITH

Desperate for change but too
frightened, I almost gave in
but you changed my mind.
I am so many people. All
I want to do, to be - I
can now. I have found my
potential, ambition, purpose
in you. I can make them
laugh, make you cry.
As you watch I pull your
strings, I draw you in.
Look at me, I am an
actor.

Rosemary Devaney

UNTITLED

It releases me.
The ink scrawls over the page
Art in the shape of letters
In the shape of words
In the shape of thoughts;
Worries
Dreams
Desires
Fears.
All painted in blue on white.
It releases me
I drink of it till
Oblivion comes to me
Till nothing is left in my head
Till I'm emptied of all my words.

Anne E J Ross

THE BEGGAR

Upon this bridge is where I sit,
The river flows by underneath,
The people stream across the top,
They flood on, they never stop.
        I hold out my hand, stretched up high,
        I say, 'Please sir, can you spare me a life?'
        I know that I am in a mess,
        I have fallen far from grace.

And all the people that I meet,
And everybody on this street,
And all those who pass me by,
And everyone who is gathered round.
        I hear the shuffle of your feet,
        I hear the murmurs on your tongues,
        I need your positive response,
        I need compassion in my cup.

Jonathan Paisley

FOR THE REPUBLIC

Men for the Republic come lay your guns aside
Take a seat beside us, hang your armour up outside
Pay no heed to soldiers that decorate the room
Nor the snappy taped machine-gun music heralding your doom
Our hands upon the table are resting there for show
For our minders stand behind us with their weapons aiming low
Negotiations can begin if you will dare to tread
Into this lion's den and in its mouth to place your head

Men for the Republic they would wish you had no pride
Their taunts and animosity scream fear from deep inside
They raise their voices loud to drown suggestions that would mean
Surrendering their arsenal to a single hint of green
Their strategy of barricading every door to peace
Is weakness and their worried sounds of bleats not roars increase
They feel the wolf is at their door as all the world unite
In searching for solutions that will end this bloody fight

Men for the Republic never hang your heads in shame
For peace was what you wanted and you've tried to play their game
You laid your weapons down and waited for the talks to start
Though Unionists and Britain still refused to play their part
Before the world they've shown themselves antagonists who'll come
To the table kicking, bound and screaming without aplomb
But never doubt that one day the dove of peace will land
And Ireland's strength will be in its united Irish hands.

Kim Montia

PRECIOUS

Little fingers,
Little toes,
Little ears,
And a little nose,
These are things,
That are precious to me,
A world without children,
There just couldn't be.

Damian Begley

THE RESURRECTION

I've had enough of the shadows crawling
Away from the window towards the door
Falling asleep on the carpet
Forgetting to escape, even when I
Was squinting sore-eyed at the first light,
They thought nothing of lying in slumber.
          No wonder that times I've squeezed
Through the keyhole of night to be
With the lamp-posts stood outside
Their arms all the one length with idleness.
          I've taken off to wander the dawn
Of this city's long corridors until
Those lit-up sentries along the tarmac
Perished in the light and impossible
Brightness yawned over a hill.
          Time, wandering alone in the morning
As I crossed a road, I saw the sky looming
Between two tall buildings, then later,
Coming in the door, I rescued for myself
The sounds of the kettle boiling
Then a spoon stirring up
The first coffee of the day.
          Through windowed blurs of bathroom sky
I saw the blue day whirl outside
And triumphantly I held up the mirror
                    to take the shave
For the first time in a fortnight.

John Harkin

HE SIGHED

He stood beneath the sturdy beech,
And gazed at earth within his reach,
With sigh and smile he pondered there,
On land which ripened on his care.

The seed he scattered now had sprung,
And all the tunes he played were sung,
With footstep light he wandered home,
A place where he would be alone.

There sadness crept into his night,
Because in vision it came bright,
That in his strife with mighty hand,
He only mastered rocky land.

What if the seeds he planted there,
Were seeds of stalwart children fair?
The ageing tree he leaned beside,
Would leave behind much more. *He sighed.*

R B Moynes

TRUST

To think of trust, what is it?
Life is trust, but . . .
Do you trust life?
No.
To trust life would be wrong,
                    life is unpredictable.
As is trust.

People,
        do we trust people?
I don't know . . .
                    do you?
Do you trust yourself?
We are all the same . . .
                        aren't we?

So,
    insecurity, is that why?
Are we sure of ourselves,
                    if not how sure can we be?

If I fall,
        catch me!
Now,
    is that trust?
Yes.

So,
    do we really need trust?
In life . . .
            Yes.

Tony Friel

GIVE YOURSELF A BREAK

It can only be fear of the unknown that hinders the passageway of
                                                            confidence.
It isn't something which is readily available but it doesn't have to be
                                          an unachievable commodity.
Override the doubt that lingers in the minds of others
and cast away the scepticism that you would be
                                        led to believe exists.

Such negativity is only born of one's pessimism, why
should life be full of so much uncertainty?
Fulfilment comes from deep within, deeper than any
puddle of hierarchical, political misery that can so
                                  easily tamper with the fragile Delph.
So strong initially but can be smashed within seconds.
Can only be repaired but never to its true beauty.

This is to be contested though for piece by piece it can
be moulded into a much stronger entity, never to
                                  lend itself to such delicacy again.
For is it not when one is on one's knees that the
promise of such demoralisation and subjectivity will
                                  never happen again, is made?

Contentment is at the heart of confidence and without it
                              your resolve will never strengthen.
Allow yourself the development you deserve!

Terry Mullan

PEACE IN OUR TIME

Our fields of green
And valleys so fair
Cried out for peace
And peace wasn't there . . .
Until the cease-fire came its way
And changed our lives
From day to day
No more the bomb and bullet rule
No more the sniper and the innocent fool.

A chance for peace
A child's freedom released
Will see forests of green
Blood free and clean
United together with contentment and peace
End all the hatred and deep-rooted fear
Bring hope to our children year after year.

Ann Keys

SOMEWHERE, THERE HAS TO BE!

There has to be a garden
Where I can sit and write
Where roses grow in yearly bloom
Where night is always white.
I'd like to see a roof of trees
Where I could rule the shade
And listen to the evening birds
Calmly serenade.
There'd have to be a wishing well
Where I could stand and look
At visions from romantic times
Then I'd start a book.
If there could be a lily pond
With fishes blue and red
Then I'd build a see-through bridge
And use it for my bed.

There'd have to be a hedge
With every kind of tree
Growing in its confines
Shielding only me
No thorns or briars allowed
No weeds to wander wild
Just a place of perfumed grace
That time and I had styled.
There'd have to be a river
With water flowing slow
Where I could stand at winter time
And build a boat of snow.
If such a place exists
I'll wander day and night
To find the scene that is my dream
The garden where I'll write.

Stephen Kilpatrick

KILKENNY

I went up to Dublin to see a fine fair
The finest in Ireland for stallions and mares
I spied a young foal as red as the sun
And for the right price I bought it and then took home.

She grew and she grew into a fine mare
And when I took her riding all the people did stare
I would hear all their comments and hear all their claims
He rides the Red Wind of Ireland and Kilkenny's her name.

On the highways and byways I practised my trade
The finest in coaches I robbed and waylaid
For there was none who could catch me in spite of their claim
For I rode the Red Wind of Ireland, Kilkenny's her name.

But on a dark road in Dublin I answered a gun
And like a bolt from the heavens my lady did run
For five miles she travelled away from their hands
'Til she fell down beneath me, her blood on the land.

She had taken a bullet high up on her mane
But she carried me to safety in spite of her pain
Then she died in my arms like a loved one should do
And when her great spirit left her it took mine too.

But from the great hills of Wicklow
To the Vales of Dunlow
Wherever you travel this legend they'll know
And you'll hear all their comments
And you'll hear all their claims
About the Red Wind of Ireland
Kilkenny's her name.

John Joseph Cassidy

THE HISTORY OF FLIGHT

Twelve seconds in the air.
Time to contemplate more than making bicycles.
Held up by a warm upward draught.
Held together by flimsy material.
We looked down and held our breath.
Nothing between us and the ground.
No parachute.

All doubts temporarily forgotten.
Faith, hope and trust returned from exile.
The line between dreaming and reality
Momentarily blurred, while you
Belly-laughed your way into my heart.

Nervousness made me giggle too.
Till cold reality swept through your voice.
The sweat box opened up and spilled out,
All the toad-milkers of the desert.
Too bright sun smarted eyes,
Dimmed by turf smoke and human perspiration.

I shiver now with a chill of my own making.
Like a stand-up comedian alone on stage,
Searching for inspiration.
Looking for the cool one-liner.
I cannot raise even a giggle.

In the dream time you smiled at me,
And belly-laughed your way into my bed.

Jacqui McMenamin

SPRING RHAPSODY

Rocks, river, sea and sky,
On the sloping horizon lie.
Green grasses, heather and trees,
Swaying gently in the breeze.

Spring's touch is here to see,
In the fields, lambs skip and flee.
The lowing cow has given birth,
And high in the trees a chirping mirth

Can be heard by all on this fine spring day.
Soon the farmers will sow their hay.
Day by day as we fall and rise,
Gradually spring will demise.

But it is no great shame,
As daffodils wither and snowdrops fall,
On comes summer.
The best season of them all.

Gráinne McMenamin

LOOK WHAT'S HAPPENED

As a child I used to dream of how our world would change.
Now people fight for power, and wars of vengance reign.
The evil minds of men are destroying and corruptin,
And no-one seems to realise that it's Satan's mind conducting.

Having to fight for human needs that for many have been ignored.
Famine increasing, death toll rising, a loss I shall ever deplore.
Massacres, murders, human burgers, habitats destroyed.
Crime increasing, little money, high IQs, unemployed.

Abortion and prison, no second chance given.
So many Gods to choose from.
So many races, all different faces:
The dead, the old, the young.

Every country has a right to exist, to develope and to grow.
In order for peace, the arms race must cease and violence must go.

Peace loses nothing, war may lose everything.
But mankind think they know better.
And if they keep going on this way they'll destroy this world forever.

Because of prejudice and evil discrimination
Our world is full of evil, doomed, within its divided nation.

Mairéad McQuoid

WINTER'S SNOW

It snows at Christmas with delight,
except for parents, they see it as a fright.
Children love it, so do I,
It falls so nicely from the sky,
I hate it when the cold winds blow,
It isn't half as nice as snow.

Katrina Simpson (9)

WHERE TO NOW?

Wanderlust, your wanderlust, running away, was just a must,
But not from me and our three dears, as I had thought for many years,
But from yourself and no-one else.
And that is very foolish too, because between both me and you,
You know that anywhere you roam, when all you really want is home
Will not suffice, nor will it do, what must be done alone by you.
The ones you meet, and then befriend, can give you focus to pretend,
That you are getting by, just fine - correct, except within your mind
Where memories of childhood lost, keep haunting, as you bear the cost
Of thinking, all will go away, if you suppress it day by day.
But that is not what it will do, your wiser self keeps telling you,
Times must come, when, you must think, 'twould better be to swin than sink
Because you know, where e'er you go, from land to land, from sand to sand,
The sins of fathers, as they say, will mar the lives of all their prey.
But, this it sure can only do, if given permit to, by you.
The answer lies, within the self, and not in land of Oz nor Elf.

Therese Simpson

FUTURE YEARS

Future years, what do they hold?
For me, a humdrum chore;
The ebbing years are fast gone past,
And coming is a peaceful shore.

Nineteen years a worried soul,
Born for what - to die unknown;
Who will remember a decadent son?
My bud has bloomed, my seed is sown.

But then this life is just a trial
And a year is a stepping stone;
The more one learns, the less he knows
For life is just a soul on loan.

John F McCartney

WHAT I LIKE ABOUT COUNTY ARMAGH

Armagh county has orchards of apples
Their blossom is lovely in spring
In winter snow covers everything.
Some orchards are big and some are small,
But most of the apple trees are tall.

Lough Neagh is for sailing
It has lots of things to see
Not to mention the Lough Neagh Discovery Centre
near by.
The Lough is good for fishing

The Plantarium is a marvellous place to visit
You can learn about the sun, the moon and the stars.
You can visit the observatory
Where a man talks about space and black holes and the stars.

Steven McKee (8)

GARY'S BAR

In the north of Ireland, in Co Armagh,
In Portadown, on Bridge Street, stands Gary's Bar.
A family run business, owned by father and son.
Tho'at 72, ol'Billy'd decided his work there, near done.

Off the main bar, to the left hand side,
Is a quaint wee lounge, about as long as it is wide.
With ol'-style rafters and hearth and chairs
And a big roaring fire that kept out the cold of winter.

Three reg'lars warmed themselves at this fireplace,
Geordie, and Joe and Tom McIlbraith.
They were the same age as Billy, aye, and older,
They sat now drinkin' Guinness, shoulder by shoulder.

'How's your da?' asks Geordie, as Gary walked by.
'Doin' fine. He'll be in later' was the reply.
'I always liked Billy' says Geordie to Joe,
'We used to have great crack. Tom, isn't that so?'

'I remember the time,' Tom drew on his pipe,
He put a pound coin on the floor here, and glued it tight.
We had a quare laugh at you, trying to shift it
Without lettin' any of us see ye lift it.'

'He made fools out of all of us' retorted Geordie.
'When he called out the numbers of the National Lottery.
We thought we'd won it, with a full house score,
But the wee devil read the paper, from the week b'fore.'

'Hi there boys!' called Billy coming into the bar,
'That's the coldest day this winter so far.'
'Don't talk to us' says Joe with a spit.
'Ye always were, Billy Adams, an annoyin' wee git!'

Audrey Adams

ARMAGH

Armagh is where I live,
Among the beautiful countryside are the orchards,
In spring the orchards are pink with blossom
In autumn they have rosy red apples.

Armagh has its two big Cathedrals
Both of them looking down on the city
Saint Patrick's Train and the Palace Stables
Are places for our visitors to see.

Visitors come to the Planetarium
To see the stars
And have a cup of tea.
Then a walk around the Mall
And you have seen our city.

Neil Chapman

GRANMA'S MESSAGE

Don't walk under a ladder
My Granma used to say
I don't know the reason
but I won't go that way.

I often watch the people
and they seem to think the same as me
I wonder that is the message
that my Granma taught to me.

If you know the answer
I'll be waiting for that reply
If I don't get it I
on my Granma's message I'll reply

Maureen Dawson

TOGETHER

Will we never learn?
The terrible price of hatred and strife
The vacant chairs, the harvest of tares
Those are the wages it pays
There are better ways to go
More civilized ways out of the maze
That keeps us apart
Together it has to be
Accepting each other, respecting each other
There is no ther way to go
Alone will lead to a desolate shore
Where so often it led before
We must travel together, we need each other
It won't be easy we know
Over the gulf that divides us to go
The blight from the years, when many shed tears
Still haunts us
Where there's a will a way will be found
Over this tragically divided ground
It is up to us all to try
Enjoying the peace your efforts increase
To building of bridges between us
There is much to be done and trust to be won
The clock keeps ticking away and so we must keep
striving together

Weapons of death should go
Leave it to God to say who should die
How and where and when
Only then will we feel safe
In from the cold, into the fold
Peace and democracy together will hold
This beacon of hope will shed its glow
As into the future together we go.

Anon

DRUG ABUSE

People take drugs to make them look cool,
But really it only makes them look a fool.
Sooner or later these people will die,
And then their parents will wonder why.
Over one hundred people die every year,
And the cause is not smoking or beer.
The drug dealers and pushers should be put under arrest,
But the police can only do their best.
Because finding these people is very hard,
And by this time another family will have received a
sympathy card.
So the message is: 'Don't be a thug'
Don't smoke, drink or take a drug.

Louise Turner (12)

THE SAD END OF AN ERA

As a young girl I watched in wonder, the giant
                pit wheel turning around
That great pit wheel, maoning and sighing, taking
                miners underground
Towering above the pit village it stood tall
                and yes, almost proud
For when bringing the miners to daylight, its
                praises were sung out loud.

But now the giant pit wheel stands silent, below
                the wintry sky
Resembling a monument as if in mourning, for
                unrivalled days gone by
Standing alone and rejected, its working life
                come to an end
Left to rot in retirement, giant pit wheel the
                miners' friend.

Below the pit yard stands empty, deserted
                abandoned, depressed
Who would have thought this could happen? Who my
                friend could have guessed?
That we would witness the end of an era, the era
                of king coal
Yet what I find most disturbing, is throwing
                miners onto the dole.

Maureen Bell

DESIRABLE RUBBISH

Cream of the Crop!
Is this what you want?
Mauled, molested, malfunctioning brain,
Enough to drive sane insane.
A man with a purpose
Reads your name,
Beware pain.

Pick up jigsaw,
Start again.

Gail Oliver

TOO LATE

He came back at last to the Antrim glen
To where he was born, many years ago,
He longed for the smiles that would welcome him
In that small grey house where the bluebells grow.

But alas! For the ruin which was once
His old happy home! He was not to know
That the voices he longed for now were still -
The old folk were gone a long time ago.

And the wind whispered sadly through the trees
The little stream murmered 'Why did you wait?'
And a blackbird perched on the rusty gate
Sang a plaintive song 'You're too late - too late!'

Pearl Reynolds

IN THE COURT OF QUEEN SHARON

False minions they gather liek darkening clouds
Deafening me with their promises loud,
Is it in silence bereft of a glance
Cursing the mirrors that echo my chance.

Raising her finger for decapitations,
No mercy for even the closest relation,
Moving in shadows how long will I last
When she yearns to make me a thing of the past.

Aroudn her feet begging the lop-sided grins,
Faces that tell of no feelings within,
The Queen she is smiling and wondering why
Her glances make even the hardest man cry.

They usher her gently and spend every pound
This game they play never will seem so profound,
Could this be jealousy wanting to show?
The Queen looks at me and the answer she knows.

Sealing my fate with the conscience of sin
The death of my life will be all she will win,
My soul the one treasure Queen Sharon desires
Deception I sense when she starts to admire.

So I keep on hiding as she rules this land
Bubling idiots so close at hand,
Only I know the truth of the ones I deplore
Dark princes who blindly cause her to adore.

Paul Davidson

THE CHILDREN OF LIR

Queen Eva took four children
Out to sea in her royal cart
And put a spell on each child
That turned them into swans.
When King Lir went out to sea
They told him what had happened.
When Lir got home to Eva
He turned her into a demon
Of the sky, for her evil deed.
He saw he could tgrust her
No more.
Then the family fell to pieces
Like a rotten apple core.

Eamon Byers (8)

OUL ANDY MCCABE

Oul Andy McCabe lived up Knocklayde
In a cottage of Antrim stone
Now there was a man who could handle a spade
In the moss not far frae his home!

On a summer day in the month of June
When the sun bate down frae the sky
Oul Andy McCabe set off for the toon
He walked, for it was nice 'n' dry.

He reached Ballymoney, it was three hours walk
He was tired and his feet were sore
The boys at the corner just stood and gawked
As he went into Baxter's store.

He bought the news and a gab o' spuds
For tae make himself some dinner
Even though he stood in his rough oul duds
He knew he was on tae a winner.

You see Andy McCabe was a wealthy man
He never spent a penny
He had money tae burn in his house at hame
And the bank certainly wouldn't get any!

One night he sat by the fire at home
Taking in a draw on his pipe
An ash dropped out while he slept alone
And his chair was set alight.

Poor Andy's life was taken that night
And his wealth went up in flames
Better he had put it out of sight
In the bank, not the floorboards at hame!

Kenneth McAuley

THE SKERRIES

Sleepy isles of Skerrie
Basking 'neath the sun
Watching from a distance, all that's going on,
What sights you have witnessed
In your haven in the bay
You've watched Portrush in all her glory
As though 'twas yesterday.
As summer sun shines down
And tourists come and go
And children's voices squeal
As they watch the water's flow
With bucket and with spade
They play just by your side,
And out there in the ocean
You rest and perhaps smile,
At the comings and the goings
That you've watched through ages past
And you smugly wait, bide your time
Content to know it won't last.
As the sunshine turns to thunder
And the beach at last lies still
And the torrent is rageing
And the wind wails loud and shrill
When the sea is tossed and angry
Or is it simply time to play
Round the stately isles of Skerrie
Out there in Portrush bay.

M E Simpson

PAUL

He sits in the bar-room
Like a great grisly bear
A frown on his forehead
Face lined full of care

He can't understand
His wife says she'll go
Leave him forever
So he's full of woe

He stares deep down into his glass
And just can't figure out
That crazy woman
Keeps mucking him about

But if he spent less time in the pub
And more hours at home
He might come to realise
Why his wife tends to moan

She sits watching TV
Alone in the evening
To wait on a drunk
No wonder she's leaving

Surrounded by all the mod-cons of the day
It's no compensation to stem her dismay
When he forgets the time on the clock
The marriage that was sound, will not start to rock.

Ann McAreavey

INFORMATION

We hope you have enjoyed reading this book - and that you will continue to enjoy it in the coming years.

If you like reading and writing poetry drop us a line, or give us a call, and we'll send you a free information pack.

Write to

Anchor Books Information
1-2 Wainman Road
Woodston
Peterborough
PE2 7BU